MW01098867

The Yuletide Guitar Songbook

Arranged by Aaron Stang

© 1993 (Assigned) WB MUSIC CORP. (ASCAP)
All Rights Reserved including Public Performance for Profit

Editor: Aaron Stang
Cover Design: IMAGE BANK, Judith Sutton
Art Design: Joseph Klucar

Any duplication, adaptation or arrangement of the compositions
contained in this collection requires the written consent of the Publisher.
No part of this book may be photocopied or reproduced in any way without permission.
Unauthorized uses are an infringement of the U.S. Copyright Act and are punishable by law.

Contents

AULD LANG SYNE

Words by ROBERT BURNS

TRADITIONAL

© 1993 (Assigned) WB MUSIC CORP. (ASCAP)
All Rights Administered by WARNER BROS. PUBLICATIONS INC.
All Rights Reserved including Public Performance for Profit

F3347GTX

ANGELS WE HAVE HEARD ON HIGH

TRADITIONAL

1. An - gels we have heard on high sweet - ly sing - ing o'er the plains.
2.3.4. *See additional lyrics*

And the moun - tains in re - ply ech - o - ing their joy - ous strains.

Refrain:

Glo - - - ri - a

in ex - cel - sis De - o. Glo -

© 1993 (Assigned) WB MUSIC CORP. (ASCAP)
All Rights Administered by WARNER BROS. PUBLICATIONS INC.
All Rights Reserved including Public Performance for Profit

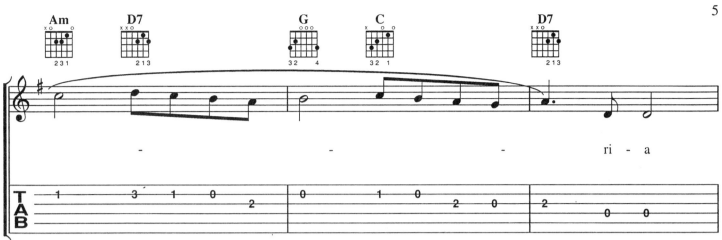

- ri - a

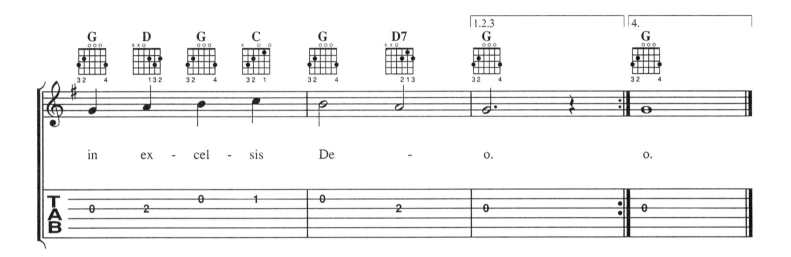

in ex - cel - sis De - o. o.

Verse 2:
Shepherds, why this jubilee?
Why your joyous strains prolong?
What the gladsome tidings be
Which inspire your heavenly song?
(To Refrain:)

Verse 3:
Come to Bethlehem and see
Christ whose birth the angels sing;
Come, adore on bended knee,
Christ the Lord, the newborn King.
(To Refrain:)

See Him in a manger laid,
Whom the choirs of angels praise;
Mary, Joseph, lend your aid,
While our hearts in love we raise.
(To Refrain:)

CHRISTMAS TIME IS HERE

(From "A Charlie Brown Christmas")

By LEE MENDELSON and VINCE GUARALDI

Slowly

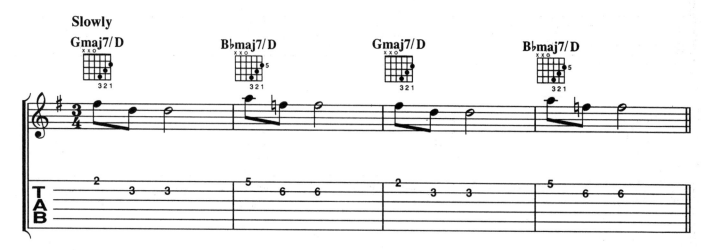

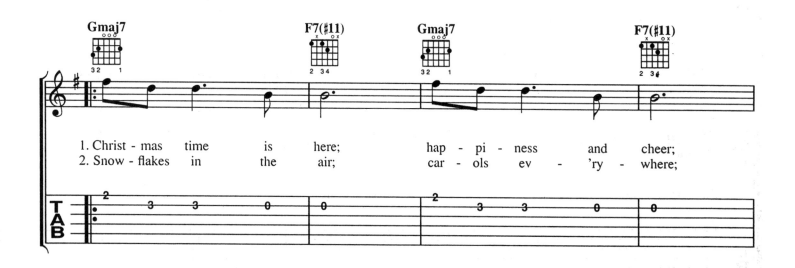

1. Christ - mas time is here; hap - pi - ness and cheer;
2. Snow - flakes in the air; car - ols ev - 'ry - where;

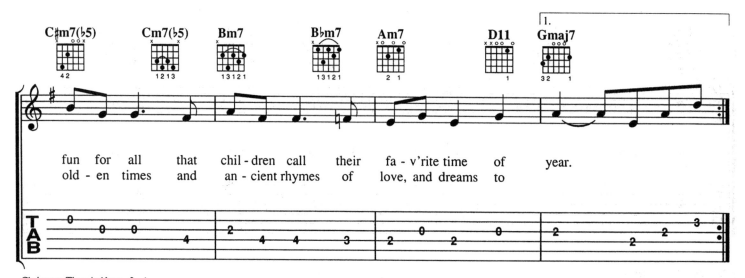

fun for all that chil - dren call their fa - v'rite time of year.
old - en times and an - cient rhymes of love, and dreams to

Copyright © 1966 LEE MENDELSON FILM PRODUCTIONS, INC.
International Copyright Secured   Made in U.S.A.   All Rights Reserved

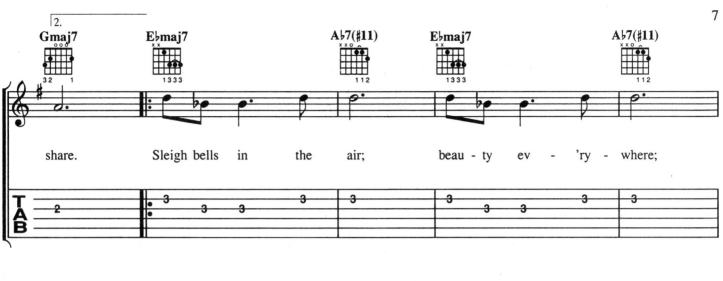

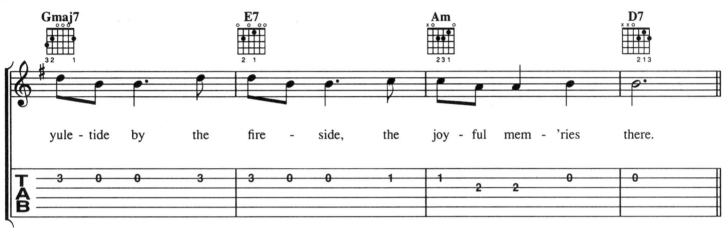

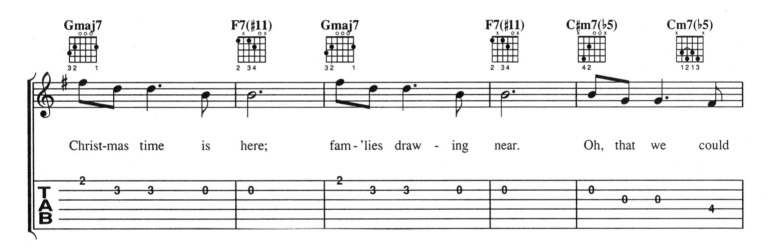

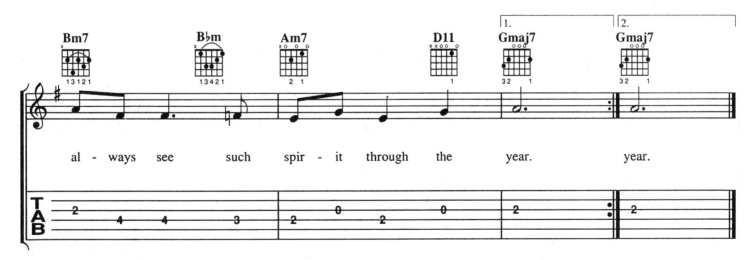

THE CHIPMUNK SONG
(Christmas, Don't Be Late)

By ROSS BAGDASARIAN, SR.

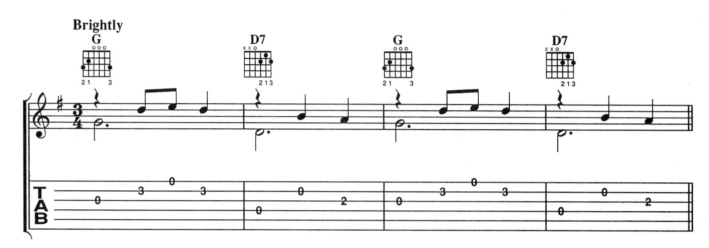

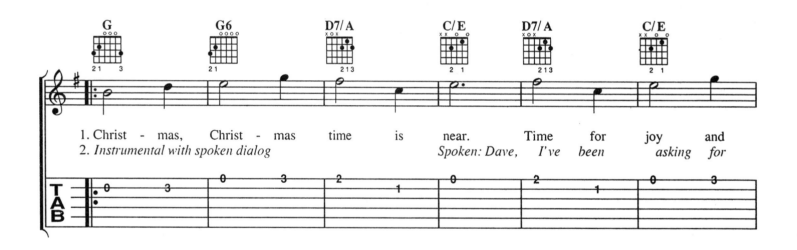

1. Christ - mas, Christ - mas time is near. Time for joy and
2. *Instrumental with spoken dialog* *Spoken: Dave, I've been asking for*

time for cheer. We've been good but we can't last,
that hoola hoop for years. I would like to ask for something new.

The Chipmunk Song - 3 - 1
F3347GTX

Copyright © 1958 (Renewed 1986) MONARCH MUSIC (BMI)
This Arrangement Copyright © 1993 MONARCH MUSIC (BMI) Used by Permission
International Copyright Secured   Made in U.S.A.   All Rights Reserved

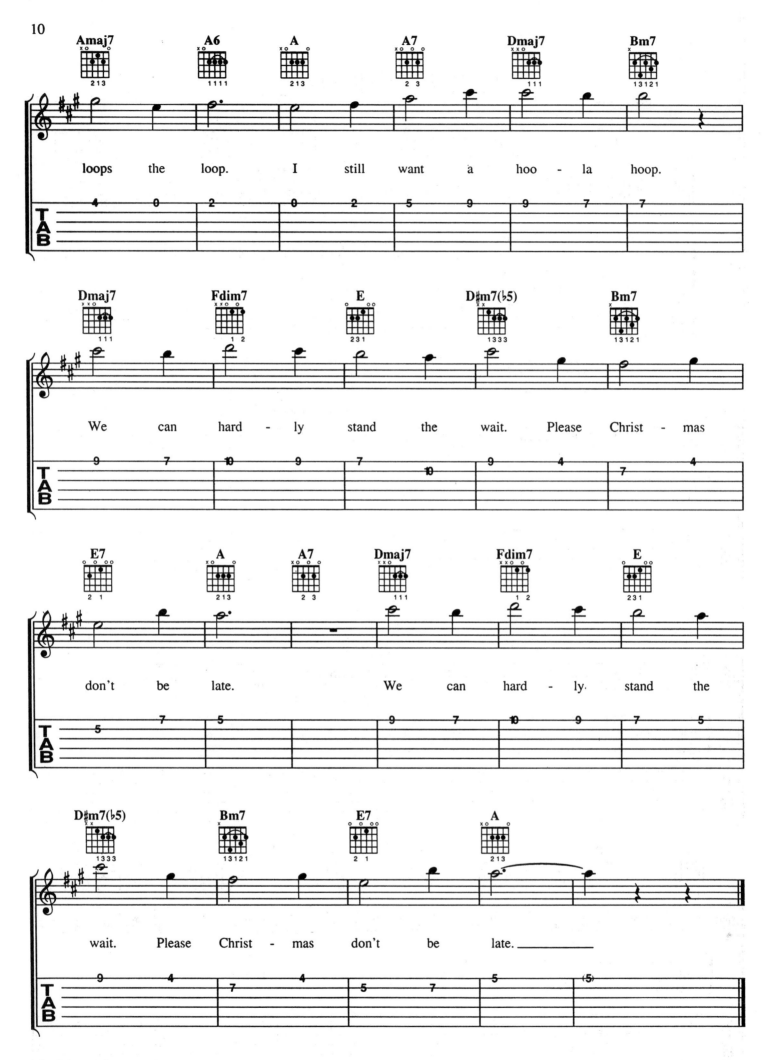

DECK THE HALL

OLD WELSH AIRE

© 1993 (Assigned) WB MUSIC CORP. (ASCAP)
All Rights Administered by WARNER BROS. PUBLICATIONS INC.
All Rights Reserved including Public Performance for Profit

THE FIRST NOEL

TRADITIONAL

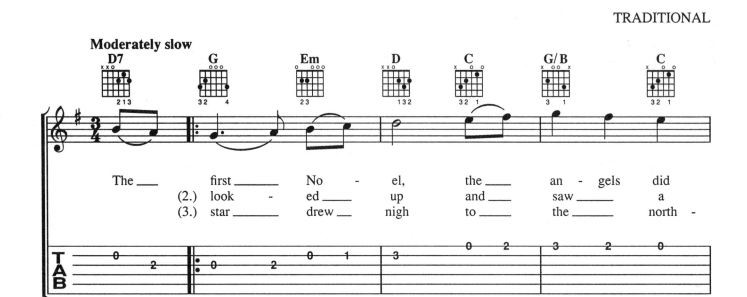

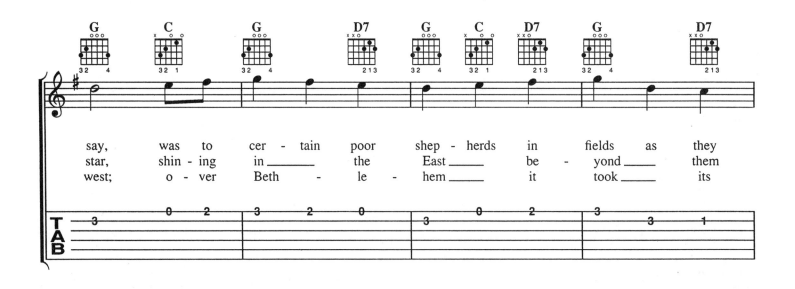

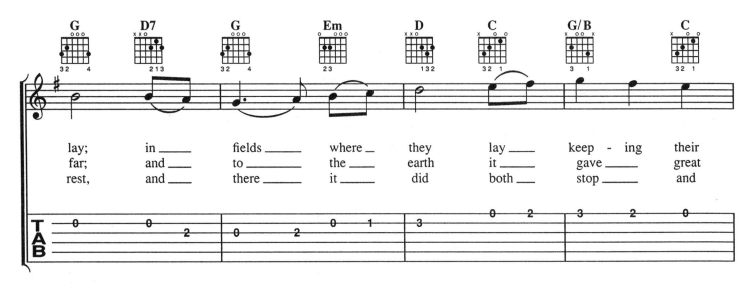

© 1993 (Assigned) WB MUSIC CORP. (ASCAP)
All Rights Administered by WARNER BROS. PUBLICATIONS INC.
All Rights Reserved including Public Performance for Profit

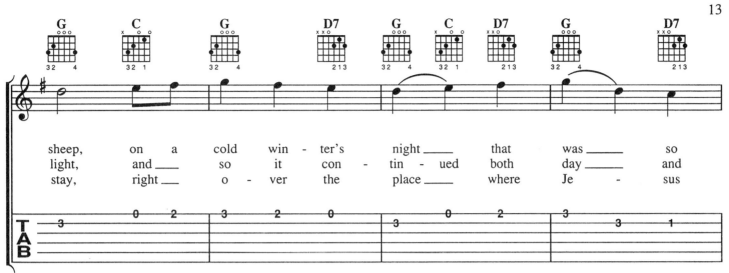

sheep, on a cold win - ter's night _____ that was _____ so
light, and _____ so it con - tin - ued both day _____ and

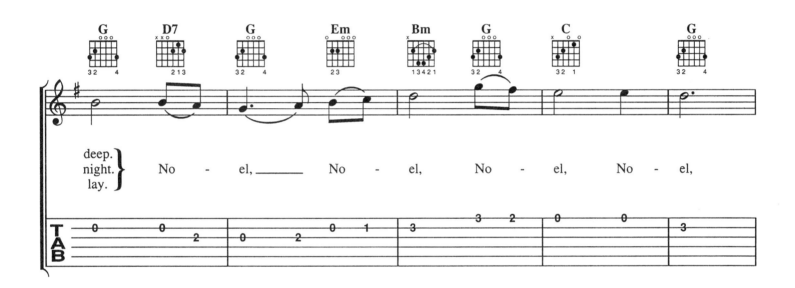

deep.
night. } No - el, _____ No - el, No - el, No - el,
lay.

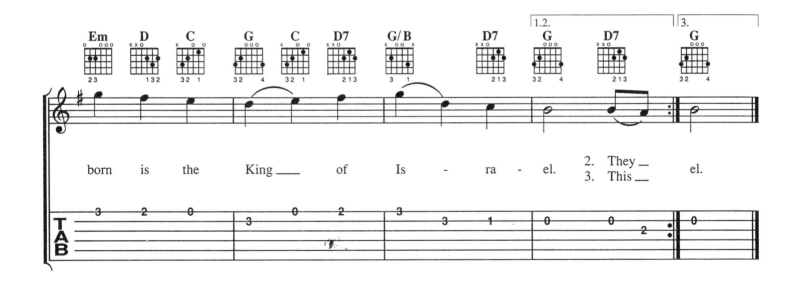

born is the King _____ of Is - ra - el.
2. They _____ el.
3. This _____

The First Noel - 2 - 2
F3347GTX

GOD REST YE MERRY, GENTLEMEN

TRADITIONAL

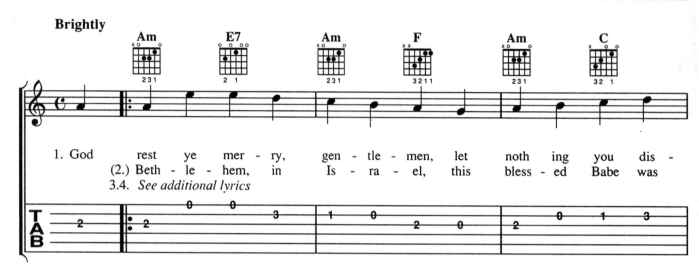

1. God rest ye mer - ry, gen - tle - men, let noth ing you dis-
(2.) Beth - le - hem, in Is - ra - el, this bless - ed Babe was
3.4. *See additional lyrics*

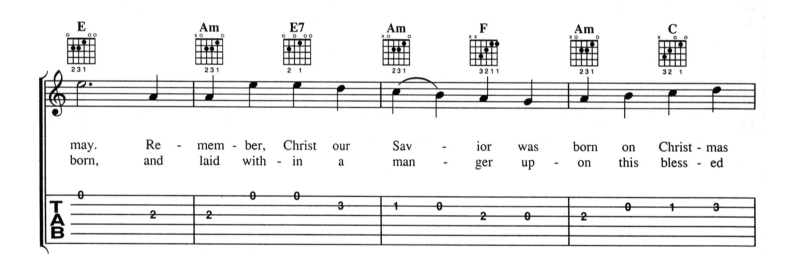

may. Re - mem - ber, Christ our Sav - ior was born on Christ - mas
born, and laid with - in a man - ger up - on this bless - ed

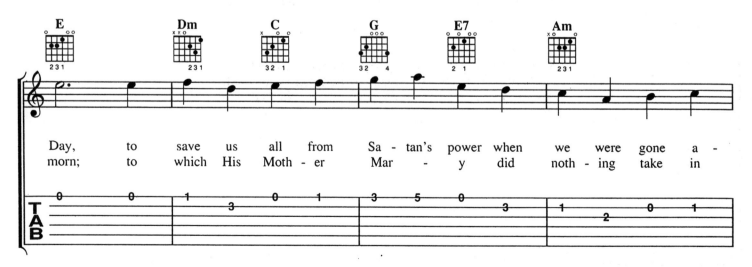

Day, to save us all from Sa - tan's power when we were gone a -
morn; to which His Moth - er Mar - y did noth - ing take in

God Rest Ye Merry, Gentlemen - 2 - 1
F3347GTX

© 1993 (Assigned) WB MUSIC CORP. (ASCAP)
All Rights Administered by WARNER BROS. PUBLICATIONS INC.
All Rights Reserved including Public Performance for Profit

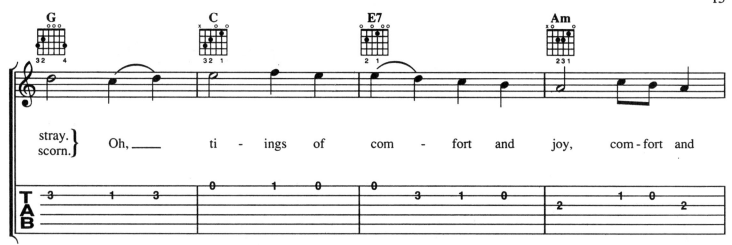

stray.}
scorn.} Oh, _____ ti - ings of com - fort and joy, com - fort and

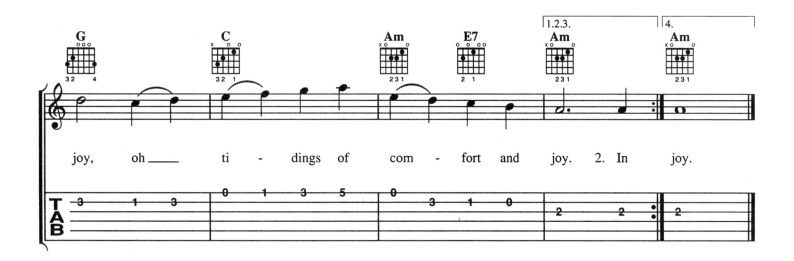

joy, oh _____ ti - dings of com - fort and joy. 2. In joy.

Verse 3:
From God our heavenly Father, a blessed angel came;
And unto certain shepherds brought tidings of the same;
How that in Bethlehem was born the Son of God by name.
(To Chorus:)

Verse 4:
The shepherds at those tidings rejoiced much in mind;
And left their flocks a feeding in tempest, storm and wind;
And went to Bethlehem straight-way, the Son of God to find.
(To Chorus:)

God Rest Ye Merry, Gentlemen - 2 - 2
F3347GTX

GOOD KING WENCESLAS

Words by JOHN MASON NEALE

TRADITIONAL

© 1993 (Assigned) WB MUSIC CORP. (ASCAP)
All Rights Administered by WARNER BROS. PUBLICATIONS INC.
All Rights Reserved including Public Performance for Profit

HARK! THE HERALD ANGELS SING

Words by
CHARLES WESLEY

Music by
FELIX MENDELSSOHN

Brightly

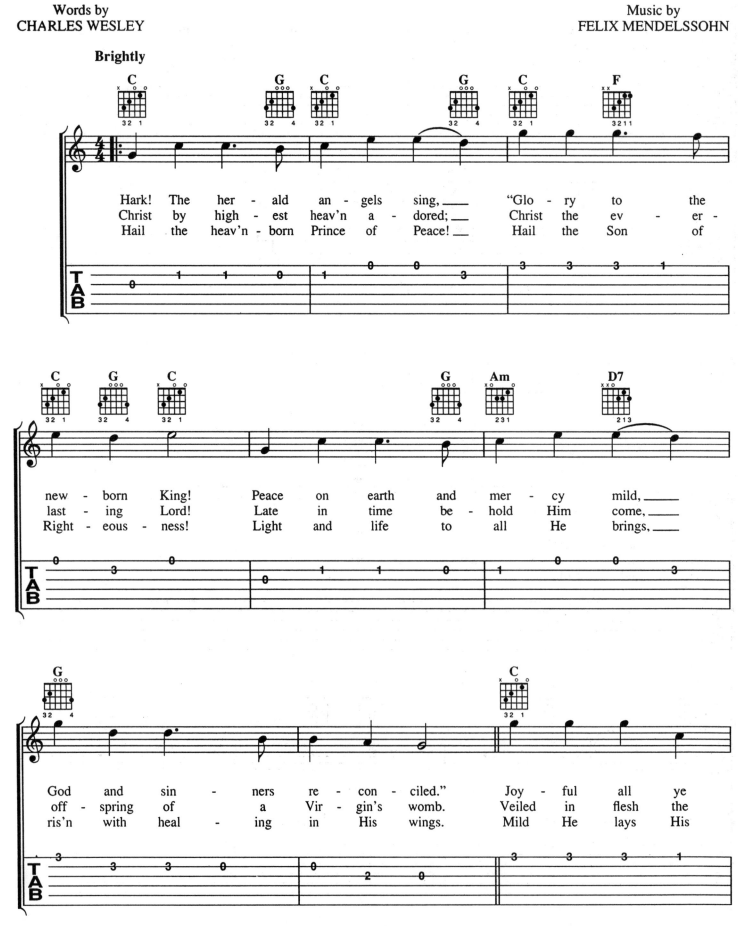

Hark! The her - ald an - gels sing, ___ "Glo - ry to the
Christ by high - est heav'n a - dored; ___ Christ the ev - er -
Hail the heav'n - born Prince of Peace! ___ Hail the Son of

new - born King! Peace on earth and mer - cy mild, ___
last - ing Lord! Late in time be - hold Him come, ___
Right - eous - ness! Light and life to all He brings, ___

God and sin - ners re - con - ciled." Joy - ful all ye
off - spring of a Vir - gin's womb. Veiled in flesh the
ris'n with heal - ing in His wings. Mild He lays His

© 1993 (Assigned) WB MUSIC CORP. (ASCAP)
All Rights Administered by WARNER BROS. PUBLICATIONS INC.
All Rights Reserved including Public Performance for Profit

Hark! The Herald Angels Sing - 2 - 1
F3347GTX

HAVE YOURSELF A MERRY LITTLE CHRISTMAS

Words and Music by
HUGH MARTIN and
RALPH BLANE

Have Yourself a Merry Little Christmas - 2 - 1
F3347GTX

© 1943 (Renewed 1971) METRO-GOLDWYN-MAYER INC.
© 1944 (Renewed 1972) EMI FEIST CATALOG INC.
All Rights Controlled by EMI FEIST CATALOG INC. (Publishing) and WARNER BROS. PUBLICATIONS U.S. INC. (Print)
All Rights Reserved

JINGLE BELLS

Words and Music by
JAMES PIERPONT

© 1993 (Assigned) WB MUSIC CORP. (ASCAP)
All Rights Administered by WARNER BROS. PUBLICATIONS INC.
All Rights Reserved including Public Performance for Profit

23

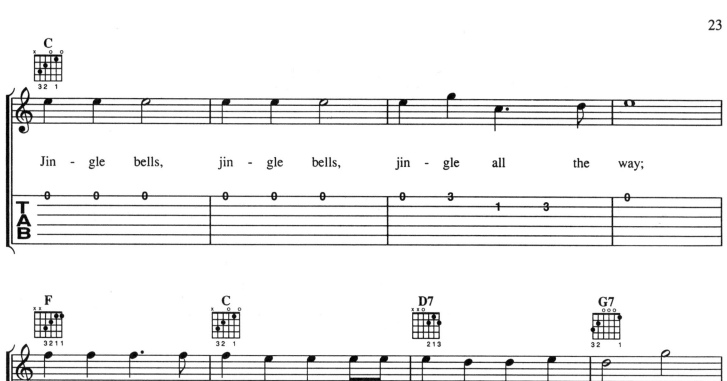

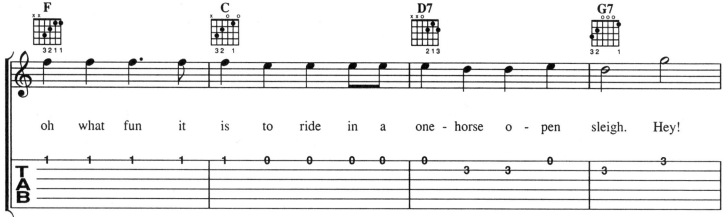

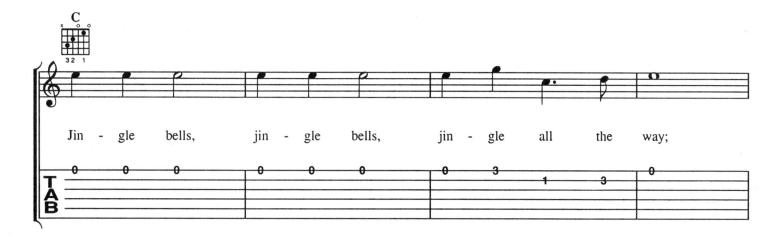

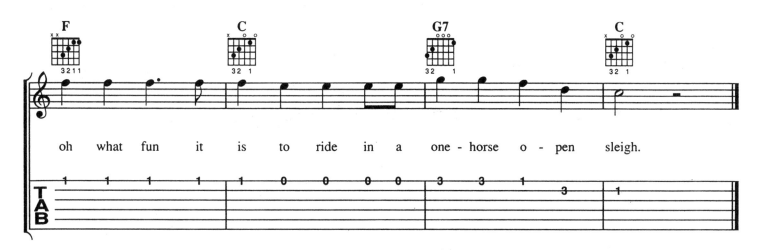

Jingle Bells - 2 - 2
F3347GTX

JOY TO THE WORLD

Words by
ISAAC WATTS

Music by
G.F. HANDEL

© 1993 (Assigned) WB MUSIC CORP. (ASCAP)
All Rights Administered by WARNER BROS. PUBLICATIONS INC.
All Rights Reserved including Public Performance for Profit

O CHRISTMAS TREE
(O Tannenbaum)

TRADITIONAL

© 1993 (Assigned) WB MUSIC CORP. (ASCAP)
All Rights Administered by WARNER BROS. PUBLICATIONS INC.
All Rights Reserved including Public Performance for Profit

F3347GTX

O HOLY NIGHT

Words by
JOHN S. DWIGHT

Music by
ADOLPHE CHARLES ADAM

© 1993 (Assigned) WB MUSIC CORP. (ASCAP)
All Rights Administered by WARNER BROS. PUBLICATIONS INC.
All Rights Reserved including Public Performance for Profit

O COME, ALL YE FAITHFUL
(Adeste Fideles)

Words by
FREDERICK OAKELEY

Music by
JOHN READING

© 1993 (Assigned) WB MUSIC CORP. (ASCAP)
All Rights Administered by WARNER BROS. PUBLICATIONS INC.
All Rights Reserved including Public Performance for Profit

F3347GTX

ODE TO JOY

By LUDWIG van BEETHOVEN

© 1993 (Assigned) WB MUSIC CORP. (ASCAP)
All Rights Administered by WARNER BROS. PUBLICATIONS INC.
All Rights Reserved including Public Performance for Profit

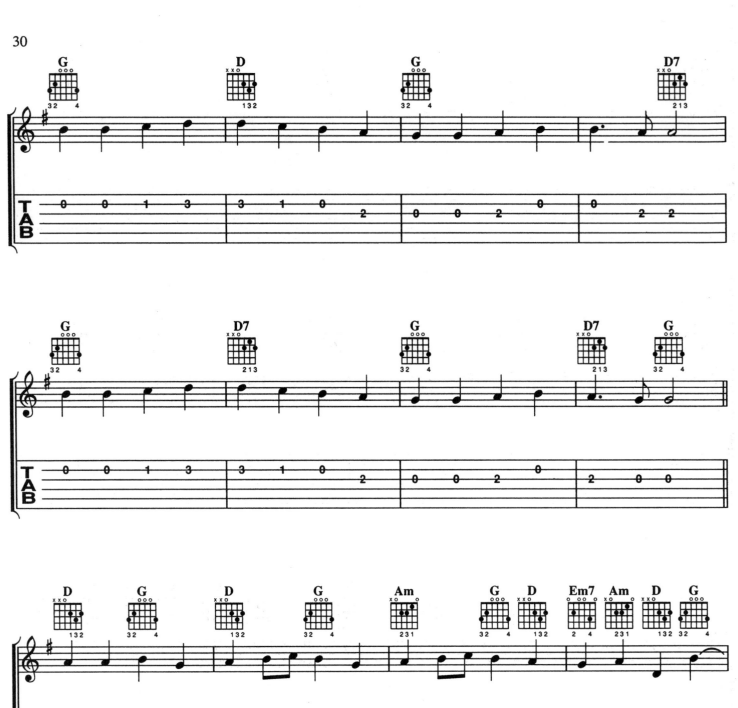

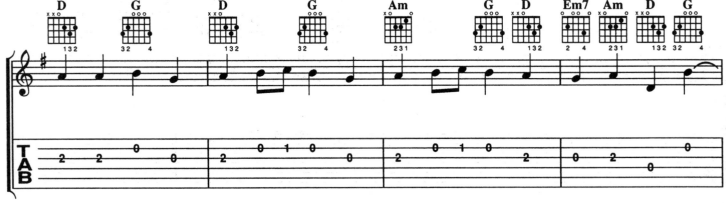

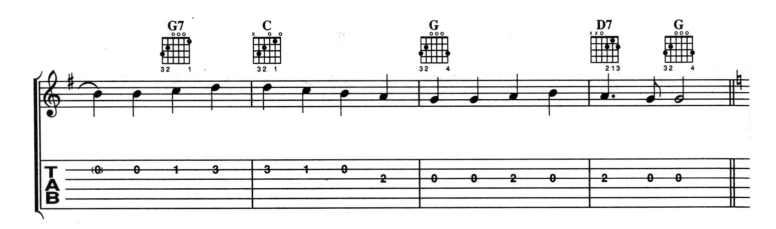

Ode to Joy - 3 - 3
F3347GTX

From the Videocraft Musical Spectacular "RUDOLPH, THE RED-NOSED REINDEER"

RUDOLPH, THE RED-NOSED REINDEER

Words and Music by
JOHNNY MARKS

You know Dash - er and Danc - er and Pranc - er and Vix - en,

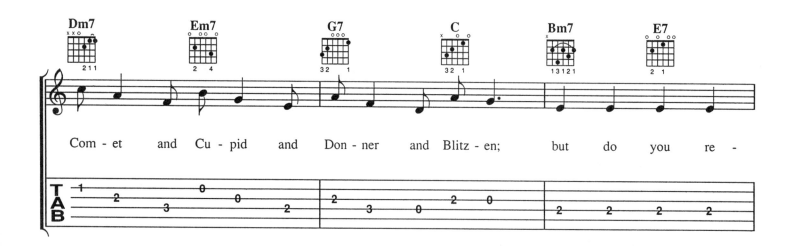

Com - et and Cu - pid and Don - ner and Blitz - en; but do you re -

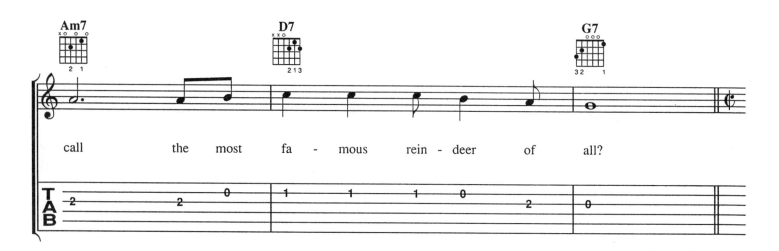

call the most fa - mous rein - deer of all?

Rudolph, the Red-Nosed Reindeer - 3 - 1
F3347GTX

Copyright © 1949 (Renewed 1977) by ST. NICHOLAS MUSIC, INC., 1619 Broadway, New York, N.Y. 10019
International Copyright Secured   Made in U.S.A.   All Rights Reserved

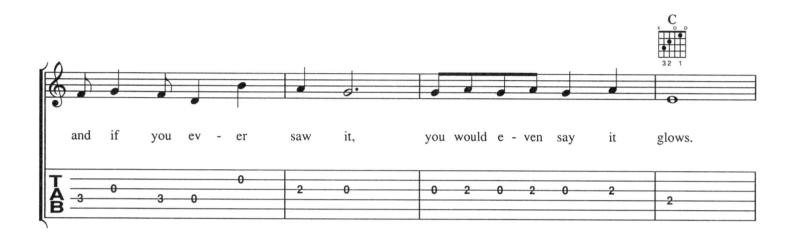

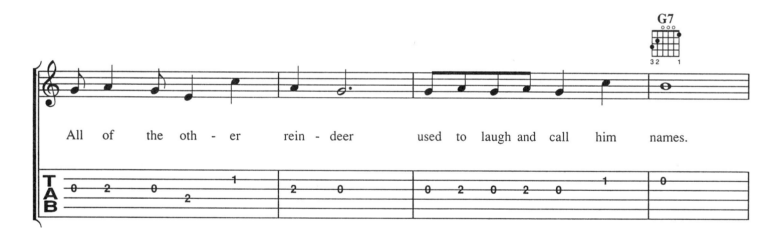

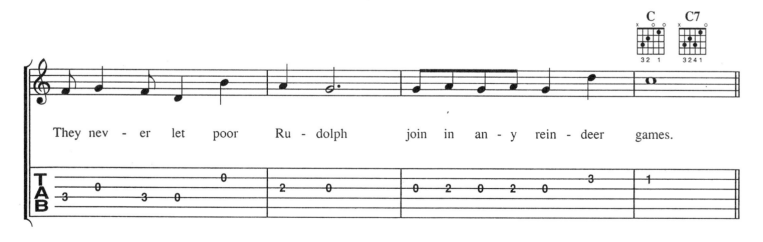

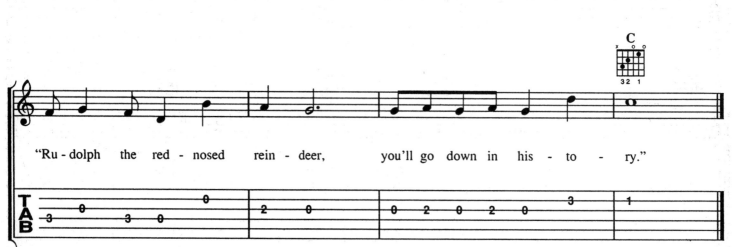

SILENT NIGHT

Words by
JOSEPH MOHR

Music by
FRANZ GRUBER

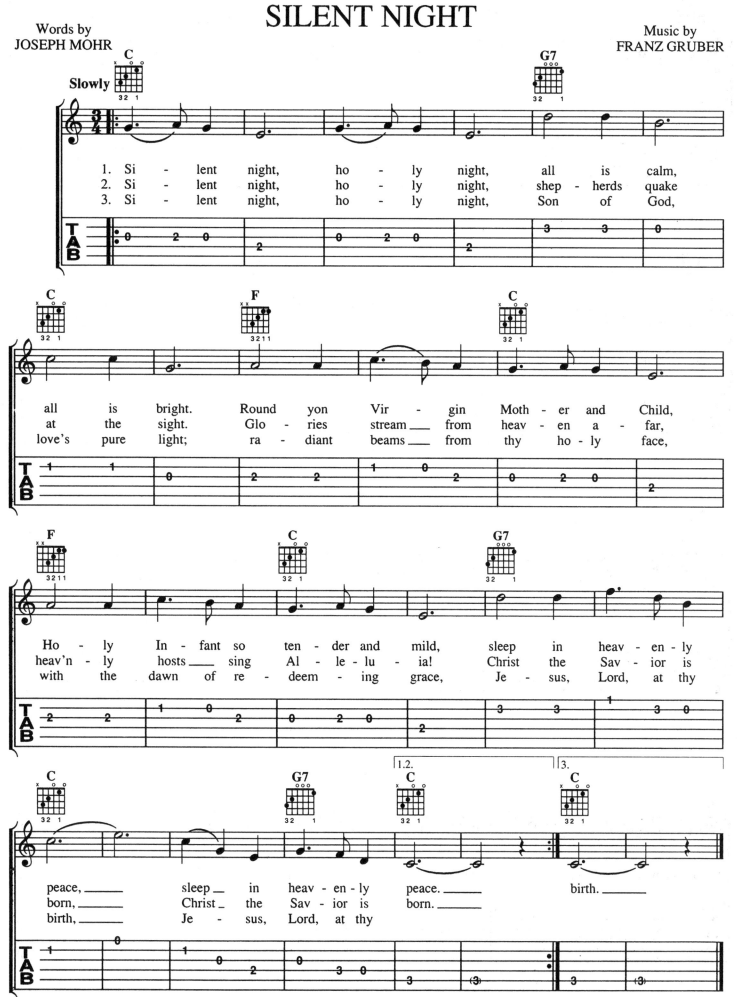

© 1993 (Assigned) WB MUSIC CORP. (ASCAP)
All Rights Administered by WARNER BROS. PUBLICATIONS INC.
All Rights Reserved including Public Performance for Profit

F3347GTX

SANTA CLAUS IS COMIN' TO TOWN

Words by
HAVEN GILLESPIE

Music by
J. FRED COOTS

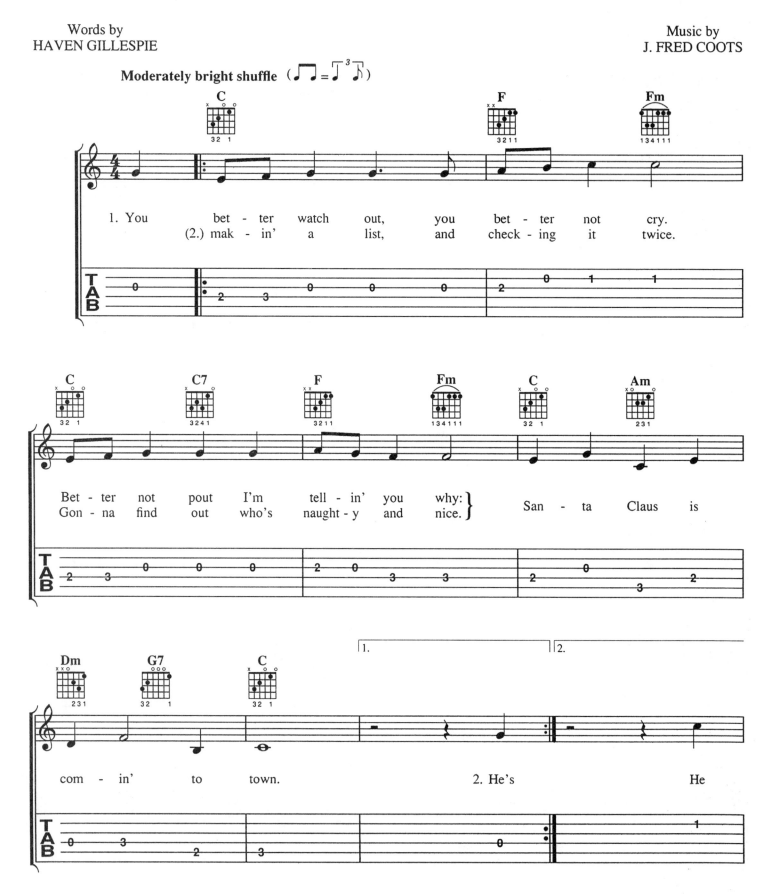

Santa Claus is Comin' to Town - 2 - 1
F3347GTX

© 1934 (Renewed 1962) EMI FEIST CATALOG INC.
Rights for the Extended Renewal Term in the United States Controlled by HAVEN GILLESPIE MUSIC and EMI FEIST CATALOG INC.
All Rights outside the United States Controlled by EMI FEIST CATALOG INC. (Publishing) and WARNER BROS. PUBLICATIONS INC. (Print)
All Rights Reserved

WINTER WONDERLAND

Words by DICK SMITH
Music by FELIX BERNARD

© 1934 WB MUSIC CORP. (Renewed)
This arrangement © 1995 WB MUSIC CORP.
All Rights Reserved

39

WE THREE KINGS OF ORIENT ARE

Words and Music by
JOHN H. HOPKINS, JR.

© 1993 (Assigned) WB MUSIC CORP. (ASCAP)
All Rights Administered by WARNER BROS. PUBLICATIONS INC.
All Rights Reserved including Public Performance for Profit

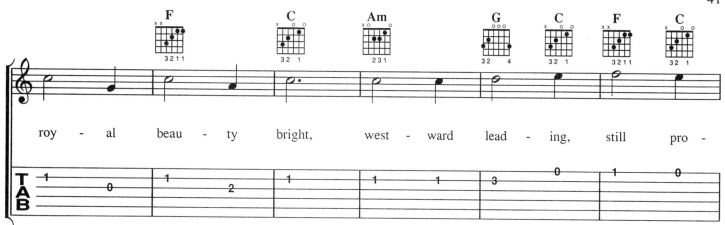

roy - al beau - ty bright, west - ward lead - ing, still pro -

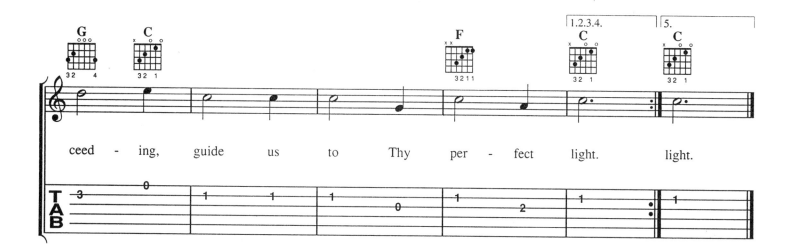

ceed - ing, guide us to Thy per - fect light. light.

Verse 3:
Frankincense to offer have I,
Incense owns a Deity nigh.
Pray'r and praising all men raising,
Worship Him, God most high.

Verse 4:
Myrrh is mine; its bitter perfume
Breathes of life of gathering gloom;
Sorrowing, sighing, bleeding, dying,
Sealed in the stone cold tomb.

Verse 5:
Glorious now behold Him arise;
King and God and Sacrifice:
Alleluia, alleluia,
Earth to heav'n replies.

WE WISH YOU A MERRY CHRISTMAS

TRADITIONAL ENGLISH

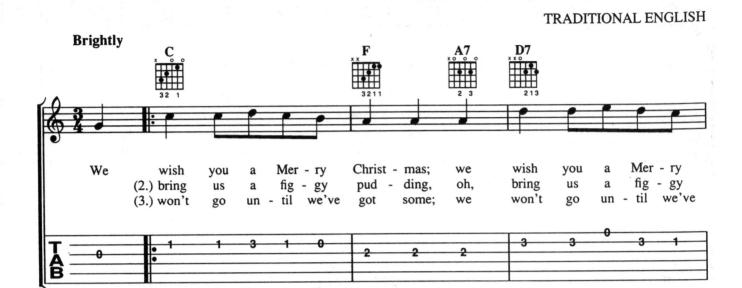

We wish you a Mer - ry Christ - mas; we wish you a Mer -
(2.) bring us a fig - gy pud - ding, oh, bring us a fig - gy
(3.) won't go un - til we've got some; we won't go un - til we've

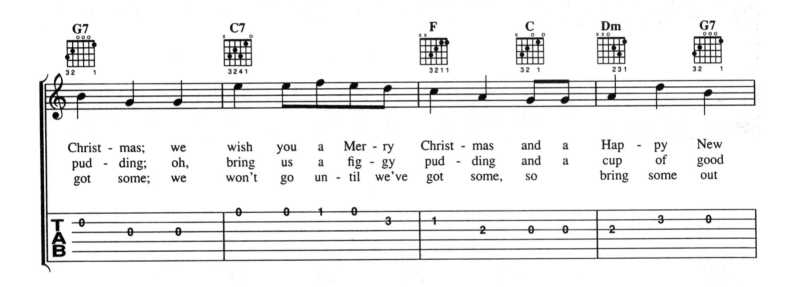

Christ - mas; we wish you a Mer - ry Christ - mas and a Hap - py New
pud - ding; oh, bring us a fig - gy pud - ding and a cup of good
got some; we won't go un - til we've got some, so bring some out

Year.
cheer. } Good tid - ings to you wher - ev - er you are; good
here.

We Wish You a Merry Christmas - 2 - 1
F3347GTX

© 1993 (Assigned) WB MUSIC CORP. (ASCAP)
All Rights Administered by WARNER BROS. PUBLICATIONS INC.
All Rights Reserved including Public Performance for Profit

tid - ings for Christ - mas and a Hap - py New Year. 2. Oh, Year. We
3. We

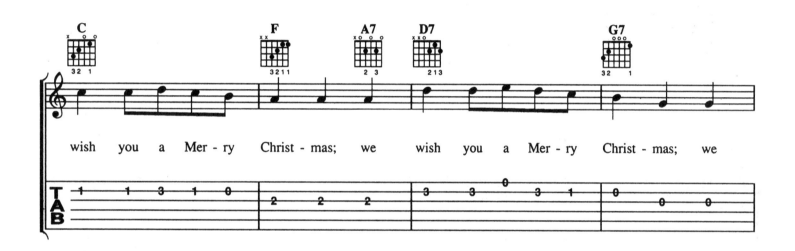

wish you a Mer - ry Christ - mas; we wish you a Mer - ry Christ - mas; we

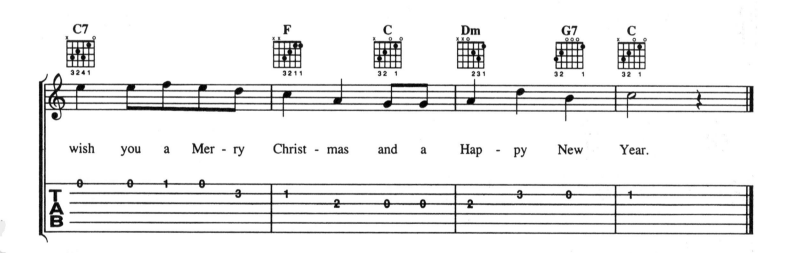

wish you a Mer - ry Christ - mas and a Hap - py New Year.

WHAT CHILD IS THIS?

Wm. CHATTERTON DIX

ENGLISH (Greensleeves)

© 1993 (Assigned) WB MUSIC CORP. (ASCAP)
All Rights Administered by WARNER BROS. PUBLICATIONS INC.
All Rights Reserved including Public Performance for Profit

SLEIGH RIDE

Words by
MITCHELL PARISH

Music by
LEROY ANDERSON

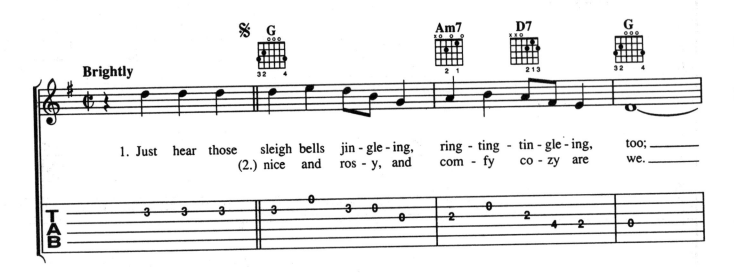

1. Just hear those sleigh bells jin - gle - ing, ring - ting - tin - gle - ing, too; _____
(2.) nice and ros - y, and com - fy co - zy are we. _____

_ come on, it's love - ly weath-er for a sleigh ride to - geth - er with you. _____
_ We're snug - gled up to - geth - er like two birds of a feath-er would be. _____

_ Out - side the snow is fall - ing and friends are call - ing "Yoo - hoo." _____
_ Let's take that road be - fore us and sing a cho - rus or two. _____

© 1948, 1950 (Renewed 1976, 1978) EMI MILLS MUSIC, INC.
Print Rights on behalf of EMI MILLS MUSIC, INC. Administered by WARNER BROS. PUBLICATIONS INC.
All Rights Reserved

yap, it's grand, just hold-ing your hand. We're glid-ing a-

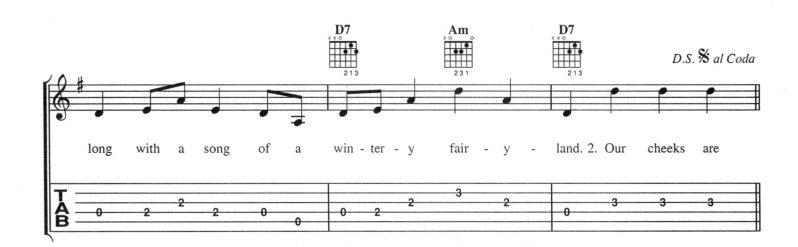

long with a song of a win-ter-y fair-y - land. 2. Our cheeks are

D.S. al Coda

Coda

you. _____